Ballerina Wisdom

for Dance and Life

Reflections and Advice for Pre-Professional Dancers

Ballerina Wisdom for Dance and Life
Reflections and Advice for Pre-Professional Dancers

Copyright © 2023 Once Upon a Dance | Redmond, WA
Illustrated by Felicia Levy Weston
Design in collaboration with Becky's Graphic Design, LLC

The perfect gift for pre-professional dancers and budding ballerinas.
Once Upon a Dance shares tips and advice alongside watercolor dance images.

All rights reserved. No part of this publication may be reproduced, distributed, or transmitted in any form or by any means, without the prior written permission of the publisher, except for brief quotations for review/promotional purposes and other noncommercial uses permitted by copyright law.

All readers agree to release and hold harmless Once Upon a Dance and all related parties from any claims, causes of action, or liability arising from the contents.

YOUNG ADULT NONFICTION / Performing Arts / Dance
YOUNG ADULT NONFICTION / Biography & Autobiography / Performing Arts
PERFORMING ARTS / Dance / Classical & Ballet

Library of Congress Control Number: 2023919661
Hardcover ISBN: 978-1-955555-69-2
Softcover ISBN: 978-1-955555-68-5
eBook ISBN: 978-1-955555-67-8

First Edition

Felicia's watercolor images were inspired by the dancers and students of Ballet Idaho. Thank you Ballet Idaho, Garrett Anderson, and photographers Felicia Levy Weston, Al Ponce, and Tony Anderson. Royalties are donated to Ballet Idado through 2030.

Dedicated to all K/T's teachers for so much wisdom.

Hello Fellow Dancer,

Dance is a wonderful art form that offers many benefits: stamina, balance, coordination, and strength. Through dance, we gain friends, wisdom, and discipline. My journey to becoming a professional ballerina has been full of challenges and rewards, and I've learned a lot.

A career in dance is not for everyone. It requires love and dedication for both learning and performance. Only a small percentage of dancers will reach the professional level, so please have a backup plan and be flexible.

While not every dancer will make it up the competitive ladder, everyone can enjoy the beauty, joy, and discipline of dance along the way.

I encourage you to keep dancing, even if you don't make dance a career. Whether you dance professionally or for fun, I hope this advice helps you find success and fulfillment.

Happy Dancing!

Ballerina K

Show Up

Success in dance requires dedication and persistence.

Go to class, arrive early to warm up, stay after to stretch, attend master classes, and go to auditions. You will never get the job or make the connection if you aren't there.

When you struggle with motivation, put on your shoes, roll out the Pilates mat, or commit to just ten minutes of the activity.

Better yet, ask a friend to meet you at the class or audition.

Take the early morning master class.* It could be the key to a breakthrough or job offer.

*A master class is an opportunity to study with a visiting expert.

Exploring new dance genres makes you a more adaptable dancer with an expanded movement repertoire.

Experiencing life will help you find inspiration and ideas and create more expressive and meaningful choreography.

Embrace YOUR JOURNEY

Learn all you can and grab every
opportunity to explore new experiences.

Accept the invitation. See the show.
Be involved and engaged.

Dance feels more genuine if there is meaning.
If the moves don't mean something to you,
make up your own story and let it motivate you.
Do the same with life: give yourself a purpose.

Be aware and take responsibility.

Deal with your problems, own your mistakes, offer
solutions, and look for ways to improve.

Stand for something instead of against.

Give grace
&
ACT WITH KINDNESS

Treat people with dignity and respect.
You'll be better. They'll be better. The world will be better.

Appreciate your family and friends.

Ask people what they need and help them out.
Pay kindness forward.

Remember to give yourself grace, too.
Mistakes are inevitable and universal.

Everyone has their own challenges and struggles with family, work, home, pets, and so on.

The reason your dance partner messes up or snaps at you might have nothing to do with you. They might be dealing with something difficult that you don't know about.

Try to be understanding and supportive.

Do you think your favorite dancer just let loose with a triple pirouette on the first day of class?

Fail
TO SUCCEED

Growth usually happens very slowly.

You can't expect to master a new step the first time you try it.
You have to be willing to do it poorly or fail completely at first.
That's how you learn and improve.
Every incredible journey requires a first step.

Celebrate your progress instead of what you can't yet do.
Think, "How exciting that I get to try these new challenges."

And if you need help, ask for it.

Listen TO YOUR BODY

Treat your body well and cultivate good habits
that include rest, relaxation, and sufficient sleep.

Sleep and meditation are your body's best friends.
We process, heal, and find clarity in the quiet moments.

Take time to be still. Focus on relaxing your jaw and
shoulders while keeping your chin up and back straight.

Eat healthy food, tend to your pains, and be
grateful for all that your amazing body does for you.

It's better to spend a day watching a rehearsal than to spend six months recovering from an injury.

If you need to take a break, use the time to observe. You can learn so much by actively watching and taking notes.

Get yourself flowers on opening night.

Write a review of your performance as if you were a kind and impressed dance critic.

BE YOUR BIGGEST *Cheerleader*

Congratulate yourself!

Life is hard, and it helps to acknowledge your efforts and accomplishments.

Give yourself a secret nickname and say, "Good job, _____," whenever you reach a milestone or overcome a difficult struggle.

Listen
TO THE WISEST VOICES

Practice positive, rational inner messaging
(how you talk to yourself).

Give yourself a pep talk, a plan, or a positive purpose.

Speak kindly and look on the bright side.
(But don't make excuses for what you know isn't right.)

Be your own counselor and therapist, and talk to
yourself as though you were advising someone else.

Or think of your wisest friend, and
ask yourself, "What would they say?"

Record a video of yourself dancing.

Watch the playback for ways to improve, and give yourself the corrections a favorite teacher would point out.

Take thirty seconds of self-care before the curtain goes up to gain calming focus.

Relish
SMALL PLEASURES

Breathe in and imagine wrapping yourself up in a silent hug.
Breathe out and squeeze all the air from your lungs.
Inhale again and imagine sending light or your
favorite color or scent down into your toes.

Treat yourself to the things that bring you comfort:
a delicious tea, a bubble bath, a pink sunset,
your favorite playlist, or even a cuddly cat.

BONUS WORDS OF WISDOM

CONNECT AND KEEP IN TOUCH

Reach out to new people, build friendships, and stay in contact. You never know when you'll need a place to stay on your audition tour. Your friends might even know about job opportunities.

BECOME THE BEST VERSION OF YOURSELF

Hang out with the people who make you like yourself. Try to be that version of you even when you aren't around them.

TREAT EVERY CORRECTION AS A GIFT

Take three minutes at the end of class to review corrections.

Caveat:
Feedback is only one person's opinion. If someone's correction doesn't serve you, let go of it.

GIVE YOURSELF THE GIFT OF MUSIC

Music can inspire, motivate, and unlock emotions.

Identify music that
- keeps you centered during stressful times,
- makes you get up off the couch, and
- brings out all the emotions in your dancing.

BONUS WORDS OF WISDOM

PLAN AHEAD
Whether in a combination or in life, it helps to think four counts ahead.

IT MIGHT NOT BE PERSONAL
If you don't get the part, it could have nothing to do with you. Perhaps last year's dancer was a different height, and the costume won't fit. Or maybe your teacher/director wants to let everyone have a turn with a featured role, and you'll have an opportunity another time.

ASK FOR WHAT YOU WANT

You can ask for the part or the promotion, but earn it first. Practice stating your case, and make requests sparingly.

FIND CARING TEACHERS

Feedback from your teachers puts you on the path to better technique and potentially better opportunities. Seek out trusted mentors, and take their advice to heart.

You must constantly strive to improve if you want to succeed as a dancer, and it's helpful to have an outside eye and someone in your corner.

UNDER THE GUISE OF
ASK FOR WHAT YOU WANT

We'd love to know what you thought of our book and would be so grateful for a kind, honest review on Amazon, Goodreads, or social media.

UPCOMING BOOKS

Ballerina Moments: Insights, Ideas, and Inspiration about Dance

Ballerina Bliss

Ballet Beginnings

Ballerina Garden

ABOUT
ONCE UPON A DANCE

Once Upon a Dance is a mother-daughter team who share a passion for dance and storytelling.

Teacher Terrel and Ballerina K create books to spark imagination and inspire children to move, breathe, and connect.

Once Upon a Dance was named a top 10 author of 2022 by Outstanding Creator Awards, and they've been honored by over 50 book awards, 2000+ 5-star reviews, and a Kirkus Star.

They donate all royalties to charities (2020 - 2030) supporting the arts, animals, environment, or people.

Visit DanceStories.com for more info.

Photo: Dan Lao Photography

OTHER BOOKS BY
ONCE UPON A DANCE

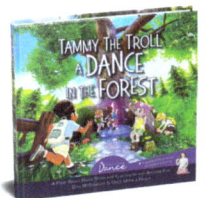 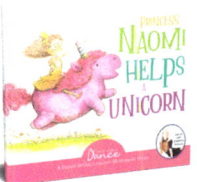 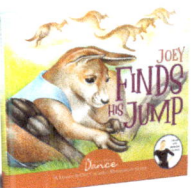 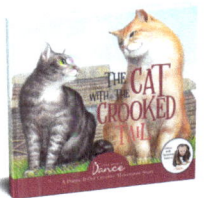 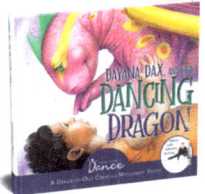 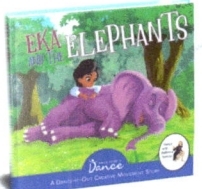

 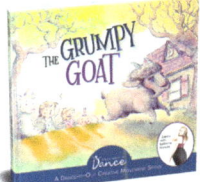   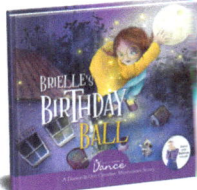 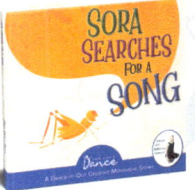

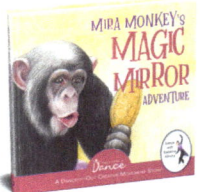 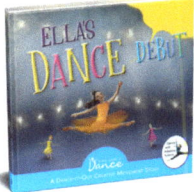 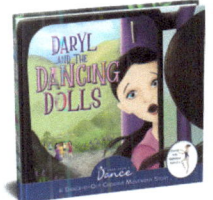 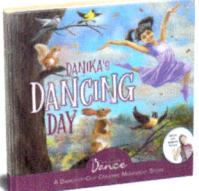 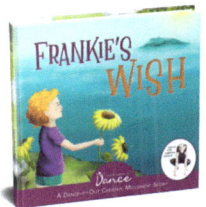 

    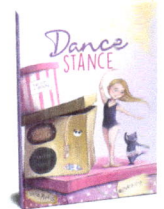 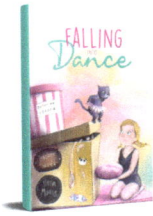

www.ingramcontent.com/pod-product-compliance
Lightning Source LLC
LaVergne TN
LVHW072312090526
838202LV00019B/2268